ALEX
FRATER

WHERE THE DAWN COMES
UP LIKE THUNDER

PENGUIN BOOKS

PENGUIN BOOKS

Published by the Penguin Group. Penguin Books Ltd, 27 Wrights Lane, London w8 5TZ, England. Penguin Books USA Inc., 375 Hudson Street, New York, New York 10014, USA. Penguin Books Australia Ltd, Ringwood, Victoria, Australia. Penguin Books Canada Ltd, 10 Alcorn Avenue, Toronto, Ontario, Canada M4V 3B2. Penguin Books (NZ) Ltd, 182–190 Wairau Road, Auckland 10, New Zealand · Penguin Books Ltd, Registered Offices: Harmondsworth, Middlesex, England · These extracts are from *Beyond the Blue Horizon* by Alex Frater, published in Penguin Books 1987. This edition published 1996. Copyright © Alex Frater, 1986. All rights reserved · Typeset by Rowland Phototypesetting Ltd, Bury St Edmunds, Suffolk. Printed in England by Clays Ltd, St Ives plc · Except in the United States of America, this book is sold subject to the condition that it shall not, by way of trade or otherwise, be lent, re-sold, hired out, or otherwise circulated without the publisher's prior consent in any form of binding or cover other than that in which it is published and without a similar condition including this condition being imposed on the subsequent purchaser · 10 9 8 7 6 5 4 3 2 1

After many days spent heading due east – Dhaka lay on virtually the same latitude as Muscat, and I had crossed and recrossed the Tropic of Cancer several times – I was now about to strike south towards Australia. On the public viewing balcony a young woman and her two small daughters were crying and tapping at the glass that separated them from a man sitting in the departure lounge. He was puffing at a cigarette and, when he saw me watching, smiled and rolled his eyes, embarrassed by his weeping family.

At 2 p.m. the flight was called. Fifty or sixty of us walked across the apron to the 707. It had *City of Tokyo* painted on its nose and, as we filed aboard, I wondered how many other names the old plane had carried down the years. The first Boeing 707 made its maiden flight on 15 July 1954 and close to a thousand more were built before the last model, ordered by the Moroccan Government, rolled off the production line early in 1982. If one placed all the 707s ever made end to end they would reach from Marble Arch to Maidenhead – 28 miles of 707s, a mile for every year of manufacture. A burly, fit-looking Englishman wearing a copper bracelet and a blue T-shirt strapped himself into the seat next to mine and looked around with a nostalgic smile. 'Must be ten years since I flew in one of these,' he remarked. He said he was going to Bangkok to pick up a Thai International 747 to London. A BA flight engineer out on the bi-weekly Tristar, he had received news the previous evening of his father's death; at Speedbird House, the airline's Heathrow headquarters, the procedure for this kind of contingency was already being followed and, as he headed home, a standby engineer would be flying out to join the Tristar for the return sectors. The Boeing's four veteran Pratt & Whitney turbofans started up and he fell silent and listened, head cocked like a piano tuner. What he heard made him frown faintly and tighten his belt.

Moments later they lifted us slowly into the hot, hazy air. The old aeroplane settled comfortably into its climb, taking us up over yellowing chequerboard fields and a treacle-coloured river running sluggishly between ash-grey sandbanks. We tracked along a sugary white beach towards Chittagong and Cox's Bazaar, the Bay of Bengal glittering in the afternoon sun on the right, to the left a long range of serrated cinnamon hills running away to the Arakan Yoma range, the blue spine of western Burma now standing massively ahead, mistily filling the horizon.

Peter, the flight engineer, began to relax. Though he still periodically craned to look back at the portside turbofans the deep unease that often characterizes professional flight-deck personnel being flown by strangers was less evident. 'I began my career in one of these,' he explained, 'a boy engineer on Old Spread Legs, the first 707 to cross the Atlantic. When BOAC bought her from Pan Am she was just a flying junkyard, only good for cheapo charters to places like Tel Aviv and Cairo. But that aircraft taught me my trade.'

I glanced at my watch, worried about missing Akyab, the

small Burmese trading port on the Arakan Coast to which Imperial had flown from Calcutta. Several months before I had applied to the Burmese Ministry of Home and Religious Affairs for permission to visit both Akyab (also known as Sittwe) and Rangoon. Burma is one of the most difficult countries in the world for a journalist to enter, but I had spent two weeks there a couple of years earlier and made a point of observing all the courtesies, customs and solemn proprieties expected of one. The Foreign Office in London kept assuring me that Rangoon was viewing my new application with sympathy but I realized something was bothering the Burmese and I guessed it was Akyab. Though the *ABC World Airways Guide* advertised daily Burma Airways Corporation F28s from RGN to AKY, each carried the qualifying clause 'Subject to confirmation'; I knew this was a coded warning that the flights were likely to be misplaced, forgotten or cancelled without explanation. The methods of the Burma Airways schedulers indicated a direct link with the old Royal Corps of Astrologers, and I reckoned the authorities were reluctant to admit me to the secrets of timetables written on palm leaf and dictated by the movements of planets. Though I was now resigned to not visiting Akyab (the visa was approved weeks later, when they knew I was safely back in England; that was the well-mannered Burmese way of saying yes when they meant no) I guessed that our flight today must pass close to it, perhaps even affording me a distant glimpse of the place. I asked the purser, a tall, elegant four-striper who looked like a destroyer captain, if I could visit the flight deck and told him why.

He returned a moment later, beckoning urgently. 'Hurry!'

he said. I went forward and found the pilots nibbling cashew nuts from a pink glass dish propped behind the throttles. Both wore the four gold stripes of command. Captain Zaman was portly and reserved but Captain Nazrul, small, intense and thin-faced, talked a streak, admiring my suit, offering me a nut, introducing me to Mr Emanuel, the bony, dark-skinned Sri Lankan flight engineer (and another four-striper) who had the deeply pessimistic look of a man obliged to nurse some of the oldest jet engines still smoking along the world's air routes.

'The purser say you want to see Akyab,' remarked Captain Nazrul.

I told him I wanted to see it very much indeed, and outlined my reasons.

'You are just in time,' he said, pointing. 'It is over there, about 17 miles. On tip of point.'

'Which point?' Akyab lay hidden in a lovely perspective of hilly blue islands and archipelagos set in a sea fashioned from crushed mirrors.

Captain Zaman dusted the cashew crumbs from his hands. 'Hang on. We will take you over the top, give you a proper look.' He disengaged the automatic pilot and banked the 707 gently to the left. 'There!'

And then I spotted it, pale roofs huddled beside a bright harbour and spilling on to a small arrowhead of land. The harbour drained into the Bay of Bengal through the broad green estuary of the Kaladan River. Offshore stood the Baronga Islands, the dazzling light making them so ephemeral they might have been giant shadows cast on the sea by clouds, and a set of notorious reefs called the Terribles. Along the back of the little town a creek meandered; Cobham, I recalled, had landed at its mouth. A small, red-funnelled coaster was moored at the wharf. Nothing moved anywhere. Akyab, its brown buildings baking in the sun like biscuits, looked abandoned and I thought of the days when its large British population held dinners, dances and fancy-dress parties at the opulent Akyab Club under the patronage of the writer Maurice Collis who, from 1923 to 1925, was the town's Deputy Commissioner. In *Into Hidden Burma* he said he had lived in a large house situated on the tip of the arrowhead which afforded him fine views of both the ocean and the anchorage; from his verandah he had once observed a small aeroplane inbound from Calcutta falling into the harbour. Now, looking down from 21,000 feet, I saw no sign of either the house or the Club, an institution unique in the country because it admitted Burmese as full members. I assumed the buildings had been destroyed in the battles that had raged around Akyab during the war. Both sides wanted it for its harbour and airstrip, a broad black asphalt smudge set between the town and the sea. It looked as empty and lifeless as the rest of Akyab.

The pilots told me the asphalt had only been put down a year ago. Before that it had been surfaced with perforated steel plates, very slippery in the wet, laid by the Japanese in 1943. Neither man had ever seen a plane at Akyab. I asked about a lone tree, a large, bushy casuarina that had once grown at the eastern end of the strip and had often been remarked on by transitting passengers. One, writing in the *Gazette*, dismissed Akyab as 'a drab-looking hot spot where we refuelled, picked up the local commissioner and drank tea under a casuarina tree 5 which, like a sheoak, seems to attract a cool breeze however hot and still it may be around it'. There was a small government rest house with punkahs that stirred the sluggish air but, if it wasn't raining (250 inches fall on Akyab during the monsoon), most travellers preferred to linger outside in the shade of the casuarina.

Captain Nazrul had never seen the tree, or the rest house, and said they had probably been blown down in a storm. The weather around here in May and June was just unimaginable, with turbulence throwing the 707 all over the sky and cu-nim reaching up to 60,000 feet. Or more. He made a graceful heavenwards gesture indicating that the cu-nim above Akyab boiled off, like liquid oxygen, into the very fringes of space itself. 'We try to go around,' he said, 'but sometimes the way is closed. And you cannot go through. There are forces inside cu-nim that would break a plane to pieces, snap snap, like sticks. So you apologize to passengers, make 180-degree turn, give big sigh of relief and get the hell back to Dhaka.'

Akyab was sliding away beneath the wing. Cobham's creek vanished first, and I thought of all the pioneer aviators who had come to this obscure little place – Amy Johnson during the 1930 solo flight to Australia that made her, for a time, the most admired woman in the world, Bert Hinkler, Francis Chichester and Sir Charles Kingsford Smith, the Australian pioneer who was perhaps the greatest of them all: today the *Southern Cross*, the famous big-wing Fokker in which he made the first trans-Pacific crossing, stands enshrined behind glass at Brisbane's Eagle Farm Airport while Sydney's airport is named for him and the Australian $20 note is engraved with his portrait. In

1935, while heading for Akyab during a new England-to-Australia record attempt, he came down somewhere in the Bay of Bengal. 'Smithy' was never seen again but, months later, a wheel from his plane floated ashore on the western beach here, just below the airstrip he had been making for. I watched the beach, a hot buttery yellow edged by a black tidemark, disappear under the wing then, all at once, saw signs of activity in Akyab. A launch had put off from the red-funnelled coaster and was heading across the harbour but abruptly it swung about then stopped dead in the bright green water, its wake describing a perfect question mark. That seemed an appropriate farewell from a place that was always likely to remain an enigma to me and, when Captain Zaman asked if I had seen enough, I nodded and thanked him for his trouble. As he eased the Boeing back on course a grinning young steward brought a tray containing two glasses of clear soup, dishes of chopped chives and onions and a green plastic spoon. The pilots stirred the chives and onion into their soup and sipped it, smacking their lips.

'You will have a glass?' asked Captain Nazrul. 'This fellow can make more. He is very good at soup.'

I said no, adding that I thought pilots were never supposed to take the same food.

'This is absolutely true,' said Captain Zaman. 'But we both are happening to *like* this fellow's soup.'

'Soup is quite safe, boil boil, germs all kill,' vouched the steward, lighting up a cigarette. To me he explained, 'Flight deck is only damn place we are being allowed to have smoke.'

Mr Emanuel, the flight engineer, didn't want soup either. 'Then I can fly plane when these two fall down dead,' he said.

He asked me to guess where he lived. I tried Dhaka, Colombo, Grand Bahama, Acapulco, Monte Carlo and Port Said. Everyone laughed.

'Redhill, Surrey!' said Mr Emanuel. 'That is my home, and I can go there only once a month, deadheading to Heathrow on the Biman DC10. I have few days with wife and kids then it's deadheading back to Dhaka and slavery on the old 707s.' He sighed. 'When last 707 is phased out I will be forced to take job on Concorde. I will have to go slumming.'

On the way to my seat I asked the destroyer captain if I could disembark at Rangoon. He said the airport authorities always made transit passengers remain in the aircraft. I told him I was very anxious to set foot on Burmese soil and he, clearly assuming I was up to something, winked and promised to speak to the station manager.

The cabin crew were handing out free drinks. As Peter sipped a Heineken and talked about a previous visit to Dhaka when his hotel had charged him £148 for a bottle of modest burgundy (the matter was now in the hands of BA's legal department), the 707 rode on through calm air, heading down the coast towards Kyaukpyu, another small port, before swinging inland and passing between Sandoway and Prome on the way into Rangoon. I looked down on winding bays flanked by convoys of attendant islands. The sea was like polished blue lacquer. It was around here that Cobham had 'hit the Burma rains' and been shaken by their ferocity. 'There were moments when the rain was so dense that my visibility was reduced to about a hundred and fifty yards. Under these conditions it

meant flying as slowly as possible at a very low altitude along the beach, where the coast-line was rocky and inundated with bays and inlets. The twistings and turnings required in order to maintain any sort of view ahead made it a most difficult and alarming task. I have memories of plunging into dark banks of rain which became blue-black as we flew deeper into the storm.' Only five miles from Monkey Point, the Rangoon seaplane base, he 'encountered a rain storm of such intensity that it was literally impossible to weather it' so he took refuge on a quiet creek, hailed a passing paddle steamer and asked the captain for directions. But the captain spoke no English and, when Cobham clambered aboard and showed him his map, gazed at it uncomprehendingly, never having seen one before. Cobham got to Rangoon late in the afternoon, touching down in failing light under threatening skies.

The coast behind us, we cruised on down the Arakan Yomas, a range of tall, steep mountains so densely forested that their slopes seemed cloaked in moss. Somewhere down here two young Englishmen, Eric Hook and his mechanic, Jim Matthews, crashed their Gypsy Moth in 1930 during an attempt on Bert Hinkler's England to Australia record. Hook, from West Wickham in Kent, set off from Lympne aerodrome less than three months after taking his first flying lesson. He had said he wanted no distractions during take-off so his young wife watched from behind a hedge. On 3 July they left Akyab ahead of Hinkler's schedule and, climbing over the 10,000-feet Arakan Yomas, suffered a burst fuel pipe and came down in the jungle some minutes later.

According to *Croydon Airport: The Great Days 1928-1939*, an engaging book published by Sutton Libraries and Arts 9

Services, the crash became a major news story. When Jim Matthews, ten days later, emerged from the trees at the little Irrawaddy port of Prome, the London *Daily News* reported that he was 'haggard, hungry, staggering with weakness and running a high temperature'. Matthews told the authorities that though Hook had sustained serious injuries he had been able to walk. But after several days' march he grew so weak that Matthews was forced to carry him. When their food and water were finished Hook, in a gesture that the *Daily News* likened to Captain Oates at the South Pole, insisted that Matthews carry on alone and save himself. The *Daily Mail* organized an expedition to find Hook and eventually came upon his skeleton, identifiable only by the hair, on the bank of a mountain stream. The *Daily Herald* flew Matthews home and had Mrs Hook waiting for him at Croydon. 'The widow,' reported the *Herald*, 'tears wet upon her cheeks, embraced the man who had tried so desperately to save her husband, who for three days had carried him through the jungle. "Jack, old boy," she said, gripping his shoulders, "you were simply splendid. You risked your own safety for him. I don't know how to thank you." They sat down, holding each other's hands for comfort. She was sobbing and could scarcely speak.' Matthews then passed on Hook's last message: 'If you get through, give my love to all at home.' Later the *News Chronicle* reported that Mrs Hook, determined to fulfil her husband's dream, was taking flying lessons, but she never made the journey. Instead, she married a widowed St Albans dentist named Hopper, whose first wife had died on the very day that Eric Hook's Gypsy Moth crashed in the Arakan Yoma mountains.

We had put the mountains behind us. The Boeing was cross-ing a dusty plain scattered with villages, each built around a pagoda gilded and studded with tiny mirrors; in the late after-noon sun they signalled us like lighthouses. Then abruptly the 707's nose went down and we began a clamorous, shuddering descent.

The two hydraulically operated aluminium alloy speed brakes had popped up, causing us to drop like an elevator encountering turbulence in its shaft. Moments later they were retracted again and we continued whistling smoothly down towards Mingaladon Airport.

In the fields below farmers were loading stooks of rice on to buffalo carts. The villages on the Rangoon approach looked prosperous, their pagodas endowed with city money and dressed up like funfairs. The landing gear went down. Mr Emanuel's elderly turbofans roared sweetly as we cruised up the Rangoon River, passing Monkey Point and the Twante Canal along which, one wet and blustery night two years earlier, I had sailed in a twin-decked river steamer at the end of a week-long journey down the Irrawaddy from Mandalay. Then, with the fillet flaps and the big Fowler flaps fully extended for landing, we swung on to finals.

Captain Zaman's landing was as gentle as a brushstroke. As he parked 100 metres from the terminal the old Burma hands left their seats and tensed for the off. Mingaladon's entrance formalities are the slowest and most complicated on earth. Vis-itors must complete not just visa, immigration, customs and currency forms, but also supplementary forms for valuables like American Express cards, cameras, pocket calculators, rings, 11 jewellery, even wristwatches. Everything has to be declared and produced for inspection, each form is painstakingly checked and initialled by officials working at the bucolic pace of tally clerks at some pastoral co-op. The first passengers into the hot little arrivals shed would get processed within the hour, those at the back could expect to reach their hotels after nightfall.

The Biman station manager coming up the steps was nearly flattened by the old hands going down. The purser entered a plea on my behalf and the station manager, a plump, harassed-looking Burmese, said, 'Okay, you come with me.' The old hands, bunched like 800-metre runners on the first bend, were bursting through the Customs and Immigration door while two of their number, overcome by the free inflight hospitality, tried to effect entry to the Control Tower. It was a small, graceful structure built by British PWD engineers in the pre-war days when Rangoon had been the most elegant city in the East. The Tower, embellished with art deco flourishes, had a bright green trellis pattern painted up its white sides. The drunks were seen off by a portly air-traffic controller in a blue *longyi* who had popped out for a smoke. Waving a giant green cigar, he drove them back like stray cattle, so they headed instead for the VIP entrance where a banner reading 'Welcome to the Prime Minister of the Heroic People's Republic of Czechoslovakia' was strung beneath an ornate gold and crimson ceremonial canopy. The station manager sighed and we trudged on past a couple of parked Burma Airways Corporation Fokker 28 twin-jets with grubby, dirt-smeared paintwork and birdlime on the wings.

In the departure lounge there were the same faded posters I had noted on my last visit, and the same glass tanks containing

Chinese carp. Two of the fish were dead, floating belly-up in the scummy green water. The room was hot, airless and dim. Nothing had changed. Our joining passengers sat lethargically on hard wooden seats or browsed around stalls selling jade bangles, fake opium weights, silk hats called gaung baungs, wooden carvings, Bassein parasols, embroidered Burmese slippers, silverware, lucky black and gold lacquerware owls. I bought a cherrywood chess set for my son, each piece handmade and delicately painted with the intricate costumes of the Shan tribes. It cost $6.50. I asked the pretty girl behind the counter to make me a special price and she grinned at the language of the market. 'No special price here, mister. This official government shop.'

I had a drink of freshly pressed limes then walked back to the plane with the station manager. I asked if he had heard of Balthazar & Sons, once the Imperial agents in Rangoon, or the Minto Mansions, where overnighting passengers had stayed, but he said the names meant nothing to him. One of the Burma Airways F-28s was being prepared for departure. An anti-quated Bedford van drew up beside it and a man slowly carried a hand of green bananas up the Fokker's steps. I recalled that the last time I travelled in one of these aircraft the beefy steward distributing the bananas had scolded me when I waved mine away. But what I had really wanted was a large drink. The armrest had fallen off my seat during take-off, posing questions about maintenance procedures and structural integrity, and reminding me vividly of an incident at the British Embassy the previous day. Visiting a Burmese clerk there I had noted on his desk a pair of bottles filled with a grey, powdery substance. 13

When I idly asked what they were he giggled nervously and said the bottles contained the ashes of a couple of tourists, a husband and wife from Manchester. They had been killed in a Burma Airways crash a few days earlier and their remains were waiting to be flown back to England in the diplomatic bag.

We took off from Runway O3, banking steeply during the climb. There were no noise-abatement procedures at Rangoon. The engines thundered away at full throttle and laid curving plumes of black smoke across the copses and parklands of this sleepy green city. The astonishing golden finger of the Shwe Dagon was as lambent as flame in the late afternoon light. Started in the Buddha's lifetime and containing, in its vaults, eight hairs plucked from his head, it soared 326 feet above the trees and was clad with 8,688 foot-square plates of solid bullion. Much of the country's gold reserves were stuck up there, topped by a jewel-studded weather vane containing 6,835 precious stones, 5,452 of them diamonds. Before leaving for Mandalay to begin my river trip down the Irrawaddy I had visited the Shwe Dagon with the British embassy clerk who was going to act as interpreter and who, to ensure a safe journey, wished us to gain merit. We bought booklets of finely beaten gold leaf at a stall and clambered up high, rickety ladders propped against the flanks of the temples. Then, following the clerk's example, I tore the leaves from the booklet, licked them and stuck them on the masonry. All around there were random patches of gold leaf put there by other pilgrims, but I could see that this was going to be a short-term arrangement. The clerk had warned that when the monsoon rains arrived our flimsy offerings would be quickly washed away. Then, for a day or two, the water gurgling through the Shwe Dagon's storm drains carried a glittering sediment which, down the years, had probably gilded even the drains themselves.

The Boeing continued its climb over the Rangoon River and the ramshackle outskirts of the city. It levelled off in a purple haze and cruised over a pale, dusty plain then out across the Gulf of Martaban. Peter went forward for a nostalgic chat about Pratt & Whitney JT3D–7 turbofans with Mr Emanuel while I peered down through the gloaming seeking the coastal town of Moulmein where, in 1934, the Irrawaddy Flotilla and Airways Company launched a weekly service from Monkey Point. Two days later, using the same Fox Moth seaplane, they inaugurated their weekly service to Mandalay, calling at Prome and Yenang-yaung, a small river port set in the lee of shadowy, biscuit-coloured cliffs. It was at Yenangyaung, centuries earlier, that the Burmese discovered large oil reserves. The wells, operated by hand, were traditionally owned by the same twenty-four families, who sold their crude up and down the river for preserving wood and lighting lamps. Among the passengers regularly flying to Yenangyaung in the Fox Moth were representatives of the great European gunsmiths who always used – and still use – Burmese oil for polishing the stocks of their best handbuilt sporting weapons. (The Irrawaddy Flotilla management later found themselves embroiled in a major religious controversy when monks chartered the Fox Moth to fly the embalmed body of a pongyi, or priest, seven times around the Shwe Dagon. Ritual decreed that a corpse must be kept in motion before cremation, and the modernists argued that employing the most progressive means of doing it showed respect for the dead; the traditionalists, though, regarded the innovation as blasphemous.)

Aboard the 707 more free liquor was being served. A buxom stewardess in a green sari brought me a Heineken and said, 'You must write your good name, please. Is airline regulations.'

'I don't mind paying,' I said.

'No need. Name *and* address of good self, please.'

I shrugged and scribbled the details on a page torn from my notebook, wondering whether Bangladesh Biman was preparing a file of problem drinkers. She thanked me gravely and moved away down the aisle but, instead of placing it with the ship's papers, popped it into her handbag and gave me a sudden, dazzling smile. Later I talked to an urbane Singaporean Chinese who had joined us at Mingaladon. He was a gem dealer returning from the annual Burmese sales. 'There are dealers from twenty or thirty countries in Rangoon at the moment and you can't get a hotel bed for love or money,' he said. 'I go every year, mainly to buy rubies. The government mines at Mogok and Sagyin produce the most wonderful pigeon blood stones, quite unique, the finest in the world. I also buy in Thailand and sometimes Sri Lanka, though the Sri Lankan gem gravels are pretty well worked out. But I like coming to Burma best. It always surprises me.' He lit a cigarette. 'The man who drove me to the airport today was telling me about an eighteenth-century king who owned a baby white elephant. For the Burmese a white elephant was a mystical, almost sacred thing. It gave the king incredible status and, to keep his baby safe and happy, he kept it in a silk pavilion. Musicians played to it all day long and it was suckled by women with their breasts full of milk.'

Night fell as we began our descent into Bangkok. Peering ahead I could make out, through thin, hazy cloud, the high-intensity approach beacons of Don Muang Airport. The pilot made constant small adjustments to the heading and brought us down with scarcely a tremor. As we motored to the terminal past brilliant blue and white runway-edge lights Peter emerged from the flight deck looking bemused. 'The bloke in the left-hand seat was being checked,' he said. 'The other one held a seat cushion over the window and made him do the entire approach on instruments. He only pulled it away when we reached decision height. With *passengers* aboard. Remarkable.'

We disembarked. He hurried off to catch his London-bound 747 while I went through the entry formalities, purchased some *baht* at the Thai Military Bank and caught a taxi to the Hilton where, thanks to the influence of a friend at the corporation's international press office in Paris, a heavily discounted room awaited me. The hotel was brand-new and sumptuous as a palace. The pretty P R girl who took me up in the lift said it stood on the site of the old White Bus Company depot and had cost $40 million US. On the ground floor they had the only fertility shrine in Bangkok. 'It was there from long time back, so we keep it and women still come to pray for babies.' My room was banked with fresh orchids, and there were bowls of gaudy tropical fruit and classy French chocolates.

Lolling on a silken sofa, I ate some kumquats and looked at

the *Gazette* to see how the Imperial passengers had spent their nights in Bangkok. The anonymous Aussie who visited in 1937 complained that 'unfortunately it was too late to go and see Laurel and Hardy at the pictures'. Laurel and Hardy! In *Bangkok*!

I reckoned I knew enough about the expectations of Imperial's unaccompanied adult males to guess where, had the Patpong red-light area been operating in the 1930s, most of them would have finished up. Recalling the company bus that had called at various Alexandrian knocking shops on its way to the airport, I caught a taxi downtown and, twenty minutes after leaving the hotel, found myself drinking beer at a wooden table in a shadowy basement room. A plump, motherly-looking woman with a big smile crouched naked on a small stage firing ping pong balls from her vagina. She had at least half a dozen tucked away in there, and dispatched them one by one with such tremendous velocity that they whistled over our heads like grapeshot, crashed against the opposite wall and went bouncing wildly around the room, causing everyone to duck. I was sharing the table with a skinny, bespectacled, preoccupied Englishman named Walter who told me he was from Basildon, Essex, and had flown in that morning on a special package.

'What do you mean, special?' I asked.

'You know. For, uh, bachelors. A fortnight in Bangkok and Pattaya Beach. I saw an ad in a magazine at the barber's. Fuckin' *'ell*!' he exclaimed as a ping-pong ball whizzed past his ear. 'You ever seen a 'uman bean do that before?'

The markswoman, her ammo exhausted, bowed and threw out her arms like an opera diva to warm, sustained applause.

Most of the audience were middle aged Thai couples who, during the act, sipped their drinks and whispered animatedly. There were also a party of Japanese men and a dozen assorted Europeans, three of them single women. A tiny Thai girl, nude and spectacularly pretty, jumped on to the stage and, with Little Richard thundering from the speakers, did a wild, gyrating rock 'n' roll solo. Walter peered at her earnestly, as though witnessing some strange ethnic rain dance. The Thais clapped with their hands in front of their faces, like an audience at a school concert. There was a short intermission. The dancer, who had not put on any clothes, came and sat on Walter's lap. 'Hullo, sexy,' she said, removing his spectacles and dropping them in his beer.

'Oh, *dear*,' said Walter. He fished them out and put them on again. His cheeks dripped with golden tears as he sat ramrod straight, hands held stiffly at his sides. He tried to smile at her but the effect was ghastly, a frozen leer, and I reflected that if he really was embarking on two weeks of unbridled promiscuity he would need to loosen up a bit. The girl, sensing that she had picked on a funny one here, got off and jumped on to the lap of a portly, balding Japanese who went 'Nnggh!' and hugged her like a long-lost sister.

Walter wiped his glasses with a white hanky that had a gothic 'W' embroidered in a corner. 'I thought she was goin' for my wallet,' he said, shakily.

'That wasn't what I thought she was going for.'

He gave a long sigh and drank some beer. 'I got jet lag,' he told me. 'A good night's kip, that's what I need. Had a bloody awful flight. That Thai lot. First of all they run out of booze then, when I'm fast asleep, this little yellow joker suddenly wakes me up and gives me bleedin' *jam sandwiches*.'

A woman walked on to the little stage brandishing a bottle of beer. She shook it vigorously then handed it to a spectator and asked him to confirm that the cap was firmly in place. He gave it a tug and handed it back, laughing. The woman, who had a fashionable haircut and bruises on one breast, knelt and pushed the neck of the bottle deeply into her vagina. She tensed, briefly displaying the musculature of an athlete, then grunted and tugged hard at the bottle. It came away foaming, without the cap which, seconds later, dropped into her hand. The applause greeting this feat was suddenly replaced by murmurs of distress as she reached for a paper tissue, dabbed herself then held it up to show us the blood. Walter's face was invaded by doubt. If this was common practice among Thai birds, he seemed to be thinking, then having congress with them would be like placing your equipment in an electric blender. Morosely he watched the woman shoot a peeled banana twenty feet into the air. She repeated the trick several times to laughter and applause, desisting only when one of the Japanese caught a banana, falling backwards in his chair and biting the end off. She concluded the performance by tipping the contents of the beer bottle inside her and holding it there for a full minute, squatting with the veins standing out on her face before evacuating it into a blue ovenware baking dish.

The live show followed a few minutes later. The girl was young and pretty while her partner had long hair and a full, rather womanly figure. But he performed with machine-like efficiency, spinning the girl this way and that, turning her up, down and over, demonstrating so many bewildering positions and such phenomenal staying power that I began to sense a growing resentment among some of the audience. When the couple finally walked off, carrying their airbed between them, the partisan Thais whistled and clapped but from the Japanese corner there was only a brief smattering of applause. Most of them looked badly demoralized.

It had made Walter gloomy too. As we left he sniffed the warm, gasoline-scented air and said, 'Fancy a massage? There's supposed to be a good place down the end of the road. I got *vouchers*.'

I declined, wished him luck and hailed a taxi. What I had seen made any kind of erotic activity seem about as desirable as going over the Niagara Falls in a bucket.

A notice posted by the door of the Don Muang domestic terminal denied entry to 'persons dressed untidily' and banned 'any action which disturbs or annoys the aircraft passengers'. The warning seemed superfluous. Everyone lining up at the desks of Thai Airways, the internal carrier, looked as earnest and respectable as customers in a bank, and passengers and airline personnel alike spoke to each other with great civility. The lavender-scented girl who handed me my boarding pass said, 'You are going to Penang. You are so lucky. It is where my heart flies when I am down on the dumps.'

I promised to give her love to Penang and she smiled and touched my hand. Before catching flight TH 420 I went to find Mr Singkarn, the airport manager, with whom an appointment had been arranged. In the administration offices I learned 21 that he was downstairs dealing with a malfunctioning baggage carousel, but a pretty secretary offered me a chilled Coke and, as I waited, gravely explained the techniques of Thai boxing, telling me about a tiny jockey-sized flyweight of her acquaintance who claimed he could kick a water buffalo senseless. Then Mr Singkarn bustled in, clicking his tongue apologetically and, sipping tea, gave me a quick briefing: Don Muang, he said, was remarkable for the fact that it had two virtually identical runways running side by side. 'One is civil, the other military, and they symbolize the way they have always worked together here. When Don Muang became a listed international aerodrome in 1923 – just a few years after Croydon – it was already the headquarters of the Siamese Royal Aeronautical Services *and* the Army Air Service Flying School. All this was just grass then, very swampy in the rains.'

He added that aviation had come to Thailand during the reign of King Rama VI, a Sandhurst-educated technocrat who was determined that his country should take the heavier-than-air machine seriously. 'The whole Royal Family was flying-mad. One of his brothers started the first airmail run, from Bangkok to Korat, but then, because he was a prince of the blood, the king grounded him. So he had to stand around and supervise the training of others, watching his students up in the sky like a man flying kites.'

Leaving Mr Singkarn, I went to board my Thai Airways 737, a triangular emblem above the door indicating it had been blessed by monks, its cabin furnished in the colours of a tropical garden. Sunlight streamed through the windows. There were only a handful of passengers and three cheery young flight attendants, a youth and two strikingly beautiful girls, who laughed and chatted as though making preparations for a picnic. Their high spirits pervaded the plane and even the three or four Europeans aboard began to unbend. As the engines started up a bony, freckled Englishman sitting across the aisle cleared his throat and observed that it was a very decent morning.

We moved out to the threshold of the civilian runway and held while a Royal Thai Air Force Hercules took off from the neighbouring strip, roaring past as though overtaking on a motorway. We followed a moment later, climbing steeply away over the smoky, sprawling outskirts of the city then turning south for the seventy-five-minute hop to Hat Yai. The Gulf of Siam was a lustrous Ming blue, its surface scored with the wakes of small craft like fine cracks in a porcelain glaze. The cabin attendants, still full of bounce, brought coffee and seed-cake, and the Englishman told me he caught this flight every three months. 'I have to,' he explained. 'My Thai visa is a normal tourist one, valid for ninety days, and the easiest way to get a renewal is to leave the country then come back in and claim another ninety. There's never any problem. The Thais are very good-natured about such matters and it's a lot easier than getting a residence permit; lots of the expats here do it, popping down to Penang for a couple of days then heading home again with Malaysian stamps in their passports.'

As the 737 hummed across the Isthmus of Kra to make its landfall near Surat Thani he told me that he had first come to Thailand as a tourist seven years earlier and fallen for it, hook, line and sinker. 'So I decided to stay. It was a spur-of-the-moment decision, actually made on the way to the airport to catch the plane back to London, and I've never regretted it. I was a commodities broker at home and I still undertake a few commissions for people – not many, just enough to pay the rent. I've got a small inheritance and a few shares, and I live pretty well.'

But when the boyish young steward brushed against him while refilling his coffee cup my neighbour gave him a sudden sultry smile that made me realize he had been less than frank about the specific nature of Bangkok's appeal for him. I looked out and noted that we were descending over a muddy bay. Cloud shadows drifted across it like oil slicks. The 737 swung lazily across a vast, dense plantation, the orderly lines of trees – mahogany, I thought – vanishing across the horizon, then turned into the wind and landed at Hat Yai airport.

T hree Thai soldiers got off and a large German tour party got on, skins spit-roasted, arms full of carved teak elephants and souvenir lacquerware trays. They were a husky, well-heeled and authoritative crowd who immediately took over the aeroplane, stuffing their souvenirs into the overhead lockers, giving brusque orders to the cabin attendants, glancing at their black Seiko diving watches as they settled into their seats with the confident familiarity of company high-flyers boarding an executive jet. The tour leader, a dapper young Frenchman in a white linen suit, sat just behind me, blinking in the sun, giving off a faint but persistent whiff of violets. He had an interesting casino pallor and I guessed he was not at his best during the hours of daylight. His party had come from Songkhla. 'It is a big resort not far from here. Superb beaches, wonderful seafood and native fruits. I know the responsible people there. Always they look after us well. Why is this plane not leaving? My party wishes to get to Penang and cool off. On the bus they complained much of the heat.'

The scheduled twenty-minute stop had now overrun by a quarter of an hour. The cabin attendants and a young dispatcher wearing a peaked cap rakishly blocked to resemble the kind favoured by Second World War USAF bomber pilots were standing by the door, counting and recounting boarding passes. Then the steward switched on the tannoy and told us, in halting English, that we were carrying two unauthorized passengers; those who had boarded without the proper pass should make themselves known. Getting no response, he said that everyone must now produce their tickets for inspection. This was not a popular decision and the men not carrying handbags were obliged to leave their seats and scrabble through the overhead lockers. The offenders – a couple in matching Hawaiian shirts sitting a couple of rows behind me – were located with surprising speed and a stewardess, no longer smiling, peremptorily ordered them off the plane. The man shouted, 'I have tickets, I have good boarding pass!' but to no avail. As the dispatcher escorted them back to the terminal the tour leader said, 'They are Germans, but not my Germans. My Germans would not have to leave. I know the sales manager of this airline.'

The Penang sector took only thirty minutes. As we left the Thai coast and whizzed out over tankers and container ships 25 plodding stolidly between the Andaman Sea and the Straits of Malacca the steward distributed Malaysian entry forms bearing the words 'Be Forewarned. Death for Drug Traffickers Under Malaysian Law'. My freckled friend across the aisle was talking animatedly to a handsome blond teenager whose mother, not bad-looking herself, listened to the exchange with a faint frown, perhaps troubled by the way the Englishman kept touching her son's bare arm. The tour leader leant over my seat and said, 'You have seen what it says on the landing card? I know the Malaysian hangman. I met him at a golf club in KL. I know also the Foreign Minister and a couple of the Sultans. The Foreign Minister recently crashed his plane in the jungle. He is a good egg. Malaysia is a country where you must have contacts if you wish to get any action.'

Somewhere beyond the port wing was Alor Setar, one of the more obscure Imperial stops. In the early days it had been the first halt after Bangkok and I was bound there now but, due to the vagaries of the present schedules, it could only be reached via Penang and Kota Bharu, a township on the South China Sea. To fly from Penang to Alor Setar meant crossing from the west coast to the east and then back again, finishing up only a few miles from my original starting point. Now the little Thai 737 descended over blue hills bounded by a shiny hot sea. The flaps were lowered over Butterworth Field, a mainland military base, and we tracked along the new causeway leading to Penang island, touching down at Bayan Lepas airport a few moments later. I followed the Germans through a covered air bridge, had my passport stamped by an amiable but sharp-eyed official and passed into the terminal proper, a lofty, airy, open-ended structure built in the style of a kampong longhouse. It was cool and elegant, a classy piece of design, with sparrows clamouring high in its shadowy, steeply pitched roof.

I asked an exuberant young cab driver to take me to the Eastern and Oriental Hotel and we moved off at high speed while he shouted questions over his shoulder. Where was my family? How old was my daughter? What was my son's name? Was I an Oxford man? Were my children diligent? He himself had not been diligent, preferring car magazines to textbooks, but now he was helping to put his diligent younger brother through electrical engineering at Glasgow University; this helped to make amends for his slackness at school. Penang, he continued, was very pro-British. I would feel at home here and, to prove it, he began reciting some of the street names of George Town, the island's little capital: Turf Club Road, Bell Lane, Jalan Jones, Rose Avenue, Bridge Street, Jalan Brick Kiln, Lebuh Leith, Lebuhraya Scott, Jalan Brother James, Pierce Close, Jalan Edgecumbe and Piggot Road.

The lobby of the old Eastern and Oriental on Farquhar Street was humid and shadowy, without benefit of air conditioning. In 1929 Noël Coward and his friend Lord Amherst, both wearing monogrammed silk tennis shirts and blue berets, had registered at this same ample desk and, clearly, little had changed since. The lift was a gilded iron cage that groaned up to the third floor, discharging me on to a covered verandah. My room stood at the end of a private passageway where, once, my servants would have slept on bedrolls. In the cavernous adjoining bathroom, before the installation of plumbing, guests slopped water over themselves from tall Shanghai jars. The hotel stood within 27 a few yards of the sea wall and, when I threw open the windows, the room was filled with the sleepy splash of the tide rising in the Straits. The smoke of a distant ship smudged the blue horizon. Across the water the misty hills of Kedah loomed on the mainland. Below my windows was an enchanted garden, a long, trim lawn planted with casuarinas and coconut palms and containing a small pool in which a pretty Malaysian woman was teaching her baby to swim. There was a tap at the door and a bluff, vigorous-looking man walked in, said he was my room boy and shook my hand. He began unpacking my bag. Certain items he set aside for washing, others for pressing. What was the purpose of my visit? Was I married? Were my children at school? Did they work hard and obey their teachers? I said the teachers complained only rarely. 'Good, good!' he beamed and hurried off with a pile of stuff destined for the laundry.

I went for a dip in the pool. The Malaysian girl smiled when I said her baby seemed to be picking up the technique of dog-paddling very well. 'He wants to learn,' she told me gravely. That evening, drinking a Tiger beer in the Anchor Bar, I chatted to an elderly Dutchman who had worked in Penang as a young man and now, widowed and retired, was back for a sentimental visit. In the old days, he said, the E. & O. had been the centre of the island's social life. 'It was once just a small boarding house but at the end of the last century an Armenian named Sarkies took it over. He was the chap who built Raffles in Singapore and he was a bit of an extrovert. You know? When they had balls here he would always dance a Viennese waltz with a glass of whisky on his head. He never spilled a drop. It was his party trick. I think he probably was a bit of a pain,' added the Dutchman, who was small and neat with a trim moustache. 'His head boy was a Chinese called Hindenburg. This Hindenburg always wore white socks and black silk matador pants and did his hair like a twenties movie star – lots of oil, combed flat. Even when I was here, just after the war, they still talked about him. Hindenburg could do anything: cash a cheque, get you a woman, call off your creditors, fix an invitation to Government House, even get you out of jail. All the famous English names came here – Kipling, Coward, Maugham, all those writers.' Then, with some reluctance, he left to attend a Malaysian cultural evening for which he had purchased a ticket. 'I expect it will be quite boring,' he said.

Cobham called here too, arriving 'just as the sun was going down behind the mountain at the back of the town, so that the clear-cut rock horizon formed by the mountain stood out boldly, illuminated by the great light behind it. We landed in the bay, which was quite calm, and as we could find no mooring we heaved our own little anchor overboard . . . Everywhere there seemed to be an abundance of foliage in which the villas of the merchants of Penang were partially hidden. Government House here is perhaps one of the most beautiful in the whole of the East, with imposing views of the great mountain behind the town appearing above the Residency lawns. It was a wonderful moonlit night and I longed to rest in this delightful spot; instead of which I had to dress in a matter of minutes and dash off with the Governor to an important dinner where, he told me, my presence was very much requested.'

Cobham did not say where the dinner was held but I knew that the only venue appropriate to such an occasion would have been the E. & O. and, sitting in the dining-room, I imagined him being welcomed here by perspiring, gregarious men in boiled shirts and black ties who traditionally subsisted on a high-octane diet of hot curries and cold spirits. But now the dining-room was occupied by single business travellers and middle-aged holidaymakers unable to afford the ritzy new gin palaces that had creamed off the upper end of the luxury trade, subdued, rather mournful people who took care not to raise their voices or clatter their soup spoons. Grave young waiters moved about noiselessly, like priests bringing wine and wafers to their communicants. What my waiter dispensed, food apart, was knowledge. While serving up a plate of fish and fragrant boiled noodles he told me that the British had called Penang Prince of Wales Island but its real name came from Pulau Pinang, meaning Island of the Betel-nut Tree. I wrote that down in my notebook and he nodded approvingly. During the remainder of the meal I got excellent service and a lot more information. I had been an attentive student, and when I left he smiled and wished me sweet dreams.

Later I went to my room and sat for a while by the open window. The narrow track thrown across the Straits by the quarter moon slipped out of focus as an outward-bound coaster chugged through it, all lit up and trailing a mist of diesel fumes. The high tide sucked and rippled softly against the sea wall. There was a small, fitful westerly breeze which periodically rattled the palm fronds like dominoes. I went to bed and, on the verge of sleep, recalled a story the waiter had told me which seemed entirely in keeping with this pretty, faintly eccentric island. When Francis Light, the Briton who persuaded the Sultan of Kedah to allow him to build a settlement on Penang, brought in Indian labourers to clear the site they became disheartened by the thick, tangled jungle, the snakes and fevers. Light realized the men needed some powerful new incentive, so one morning he called them together and, as they watched, filled a large cannon with silver dollars and fired it straight into the trees. The Indians seized their axes and cleared the jungle so fast that, only days later, work could be started on the wharves, roads and houses of this hot little place that had just become the newest fragment of Empire.

Flight MH 350 to Kota Bharu, operated by a Malaysian Airlines System 737, was scheduled to depart from Penang at 1750. During the day I made a number of phone calls, looking for anyone who could tell me about the pre-war local aviation picture, but none of the people I spoke to seemed even to know what I was talking about. In the Anchor Bar before lunch an affable young Malaysian who worked for Wira Kris, a charter company operating a fleet of light aircraft, explained, 'Everyone in the aviation business here is young. Older people like to have a quiet life, so they leave. The competition for aviation jobs is very big – for flying or ground duties they take only the best graduates, and students. They must also be good physical specimens, strong and fit, very sporty. It is Malaysia's most high-profile profession.'

I decided to go to the airport early and try my luck there; perhaps I would come across someone furtively concealing the onset of a middle-age spread who would at least acknowledge the existence of the past. While packing my bag I decided to jettison half a dozen cotton vests and a heavy woollen sweater brought along for chilly evenings in northern India. I offered them to the room boy who beamed and thanked me effusively. 'But you must write chitty or management will say I have stolen these goods.'

'All right.' I picked up my notebook. 'What shall I say?'

He frowned and cleared his throat. 'Put: "I give six white singlets and a green jumper, army-style, of my own free will to Room Boy Mohammed."'

I dated the document and handed it over. He took the clothing and dashed out, but returned a moment later holding a folding Chinese paper fan delicately painted with swallows and willows. 'It is for your mem,' he said. 'You please tell her it is from Mohammed at E. & O.'

Half an hour later I arrived back at the Bayan Lepas terminal, the gaudy tiles on that lofty longhouse roof taking on the patina of silk in the late-afternoon sun. Inside I made a few random inquiries, but all the responsible persons I spoke to looked like teenage marathon runners and seemed unaware of any significant airline operations that pre-dated the invention of the jet engine. Out on the tarmac squads of pubescent girl air cadets in short blue tunics were drilling beside three parked Shorts Skyvans, arms swinging, knees scrubbed, faces shining with effort as they wheeled, turned, marched and counter-marched, gravely preparing to become the aircrew and ground personnel of the next generation. I gave up and retired to the departure lounge.

It was only when I reached Singapore, several days later, that I finally tracked down a veteran who had worked in Penang during the Imperial era – and whose memories therefore belong in this section of the narrative. Harold J. Foley, a retired Principal Officer of the Singapore Prison Service, was a tall, shy, courteous man who lived with his wife Milly in a suburban bungalow surrounded by a small, vivid garden. As Milly brought glasses of fresh lime juice her husband said he had been the chief air-traffic controller at Penang when it was the only airport in Malaya with night-landing facilities. 'At first there was just a gas beacon burning on the hillside above the strip – good for picking up Penang in the dark but no real use otherwise. Then they installed boundary lights and special searchlights for illuminating the runway. I first went there to work on the construction of the aerodrome but in 1936 they sent me to the UK for air traffic training – I did the theory course at Hurn, the practical at Manchester Ringway – then they appointed me ATC officer at a salary of forty Straits dollars a month and gave me a radio, an Aldis lamp and two local assistants. I was as happy as a sandboy but no slackness was tolerated in my tower. There are dangerous hills around Bayan Lepas and they kept us on our toes. Is your drink sweet enough? Does it need a little more sugar? Milly can bring it.'

I assured him the drink was excellent.

'We like our lime juice tart,' said Mr Foley.

I asked him what other personnel had been employed at Bayan Lepas.

'We had a little Customs and Immigration Department. There were a dozen traffic hands who did the manual work, cutting the grass, loading and unloading aircraft. The refuelling was done by the chaps who drove the old Shell and Esso tankers, and the E. & O. provided the inflight catering. They sent out drinks and boxes of *excellent* sandwiches. The traffic hands were supposed to put them aboard the aircraft but quite often they took them around the back of the hangar to sample them first and angry scenes with the Imperial and KLM stewards would follow. I am not judging the traffic hands; I have to admit that some of those sandwiches also found their way up to the control tower.' He grinned. 'The main user of Penang then was Wern's Air Services, a local company that flew Rapides down to Singapore and employed a Penang girl as an air hostess. The trip took just over three hours. KLM came through twice a week, their overnight service from Jakarta arriving at 0730 hours precisely. It didn't matter how bad the conditions were, those pilots always touched down right on the button. I met them all because they reported to me for their onward weather. Smirnoff was a big solid chap with no small talk and a faraway look in his eyes. In his thoughts he sort of seemed to be somewhere else. You often find that with exiles, but I never knew whether he was dreaming about Russia or about just getting back into the sky again; Smirnoff never looked too comfortable with his feet on the ground. I knew Parmentier, too, and Moll, his co-pilot. Parmentier was always correct, always neat in his white shirt and dark trousers even if he had spent the night flying blind through a typhoon. Once I flew down to Singapore in Parmentier's DC2. It was a stormy day and probably the bumpiest journey I ever made, but I felt no fear. We hit one particular air pocket that seemed to reach right down to the ground. It was a hell of a fall but as we dropped I remember thinking we'd be okay because this man *couldn't crash*.'

I asked Mr Foley about the Imperial men. 'Ah, the Atalanta pilots,' he said. 'Well, there was Captain Alderson, a nice chap who always liked a chat. And Captain Mollard, who knew this part of the world so well he could have flown over it blindfolded. And Captain Locke – he was like a Dutchman, no fuss, very professional, always landing at 0200 prompt, refuelling, getting his weather and taking straight off again for Singapore – and Captain Paine, who was always late. He flew the Empire boats which landed at Glugor and were also my responsibility. My job was to prepare the flare path for night landings. The flares were kerosene lamps stuck on top of four-foot-high floats. We lit them with matches and dropped them off the back of a fast pinnace along a 1,200-yard stretch with searchlight boats stationed at both ends. We had already picked up the skipper on radio 100 miles out and, when he was overhead, he'd circle until I signalled him with my Aldis lamp. He acknowledged by flashing his landing lights. If we suddenly spotted an obstruction, a fishing junk or a floating log – we always swept the track first, and those last-minute alarms were a real nightmare – I fired a red Very light telling him to abort. The Imperial boats arrived at midnight and left again at 0300 sharp; they had to be in Singapore in time for breakfast at Raffles and, while the Shell tanker launch did the refuelling, Mansfield's, the Penang agents, brought the passengers ashore for a cup of tea. I didn't have much to do with them. All I remember is that they were confident, well-dressed people who behaved as if they had plenty of money.'

Then, gradually, the tenor of life began to change. When an RAF Sunderland flying boat – the Service version of the Empire – was forced down in the sea sixty miles off Penang while searching for survivors from two Wildebeest bombers that had collided near Alor Setar, Mr Foley was ordered out in his pinnace to find it. The Sunderland, suffering from overheated engines, was able to follow him home to Glugor, rumbling along through an oily swell under its own power.

As the Japanese invasion force closed on Penang the Singapore authorities ordered him to abandon Bayan Lepas. He disobeyed. 'The Japs had already bombed Butterworth on the mainland so I knew ours was the only serviceable strip in the area and I reckoned it had to be kept open. All my staff left, except for one Indian assistant I had looked after as a boy. They called us fools. Then, at midday on 11 December 1941 – it was my wife's birthday; *everything* always happens on Milly's birthday – a flight of twelve fighters suddenly appeared over the field. We thought it was the RAF and ran out to wave but, of course, they were Zeros. It was very noisy and frightening. They fired several thousand rounds but the only damage they did was to kill a cow. The Indian and I stayed for another six days, living on biscuits, but there were no more attacks. Then someone told us the RAF had gone to Singapore. There was no more point in staying so we went into George Town, collecting Milly from the telephone exchange where she worked, and

caught the last train out of Butterworth. I was working in the control tower at Kallang, the new Singapore airport, when the city fell. The Japanese sent me back to Penang. Things were very bad there. Four of my brothers were getting the water treatment in the George Town jail – they made you drink a lot then jumped on your stomach – and one died. I was not sent to the jail but I had to kneel in front of Suzuki, the famous headcutter, who hit me with judo blows. I can remember thinking I must not tell Milly; she hated the Japs and would really have gone for Suzuki. But I survived and thought, well, this is not for me, so I left and went up a hill. I had a friend on the hill and for the rest of the war I just lived there quietly. When we heard the Japs had surrendered I came down again and went back to my tower at Bayan Lepas. Once again it was business as usual.'

Now, almost forty years later, the passengers for the MAS flight to Kota Bharu were filing into the departure lounge, only a few yards from the site of Harold Foley's old tower. People spoke in murmurs and the loudest sounds were the barked commands from the wiry, bespectacled woman drilling the girls out on the apron. I wandered into the bookshop, its shelves stacked with paperbacks on self-improvement: *How to be a Better Manager, Success in Financial Accounting, Play Snooker Like a Champ, Who Wants to be a Millionaire?, Win at Tennis, Investing Your Nest Egg, How to Make Your Own Luck* and *Get That Job!*

The flight was called. We filed through the airbridge into a 737 where the stewardesses, beautiful, strong-looking graduates of the air-cadet training scheme, strode up and down the aisles, checking our seat belts and snapping the overhead lockers 37 shut. The little Boeing took off precisely on time, its port wing-tip seeming almost to brush a lofty green hill as it scrambled into the sky. The noise and rush of our passage brought hundreds of startled white birds tumbling out of the forest. They swirled away like confetti as we climbed towards Butterworth, passed Grik and headed out across the green escarpments and bright red earth of Malaysia. The stewardesses brought coffee and sweet yellow cake. We bumped over the dimpled topography of the highlands and, only a few minutes into the half-hour flight, I picked up the South China Sea ahead on the other coast, glassy in the late afternoon sun. The young man in the neighbouring seat, a dental student, told me that Kota Bharu was the home of the previous king. 'He is the Sultan of Kelantan. In Malaysia the king changes every five years. There are nine sultans and they themselves elect the new king. So everyone has a turn. It is very democratic. That way the king does not get too many big ideas.'

With the spoilers out and the engines throttled back we drifted across a bright river estuary scattered with islands, our shadow slipping between those cast by the triangular patchwork sails of small fishing craft. There were settlements on both banks. The estuary split and ran out to the sea through a bewildering number of channels which merged into a watery, palm-fringed horizon as we sank towards Pengkalan Chepa airport. An uncommunicative old man drove me through coconut groves to the Perdana Hotel, its swimming pool filled with shouting, splashing children. I had grilled mackerel for dinner, caught that day, and a pudding made from jackfruit. In the bar a young Malaysian pianist in a dinner jacket was playing requests. An American couple asked him for a Chopin nocturne which he knocked off between 'Amor' and 'Light My Fire'. There were some pretty girls in the bar, looking for action. I talked to a local businessman who said that Kota Bharu had two famous beaches. The first was called Pantai Chinta Berahi, or The Beach of Passionate Love, and the second Pantai Dasar Sabak. It was here, at 16.55 GMT on 7 December 1941, ninety-five minutes before the attack on Pearl Harbor, that the Imperial Japanese Forces entered the Second World War, landing with their bicycles and pedalling off down the long road to Singapore. When I left the bar the pianist was playing 'The Moonlight Sonata'.

On the way back to Pengkalan Chepa at 6.30 next morning my driver suddenly halted his rattling Toyota by a small kampong and wound down the window. It was still dark and the air held a sharp night chill. 'Listen,' he commanded and I heard, coming from the shadowy kampong, a bird singing with extraordinary power and sweetness. Its rich, liquid voice flooded through the car as though amplified by quadrophonic speakers. 'That is a *merbok*,' said the driver. 'We catch them in the forest and train them for big competition in June. Early morning is best time for *merbok* practice. Now they are singing all over Kota Bharu.'

The check-in hall in Pengkalan Chepa's little terminal was open to the road. Half a dozen figures sat sleepily, waiting for the flight to Alor Setar – or, as it is more colloquially known, Alor Star. The terminal signs were all in Bahasa Malaysia and, emerging from the Gents, or *Tandas Lelaki*, I glimpsed through the half-drawn curtain of the prayer room a kneeling man in a smart white suit muttering and agitatedly polishing his spectacles. We were directed to the flight through *Pintu A*. The 737 was sitting out on the empty apron with its lights on, humming comfortably and ready to go.

We took off through rolling banks of sea mist. The atmosphere at the rear of the aircraft, where I sat, was as clubby and convivial as a tea house. My neighbour slipped off his sandals and massaged his feet while he chatted animatedly with his friends. Half the thirty-five-minute flight was made across the protruding southernmost tip of Thailand; we passed back into Malaysian airspace near Kampung Pinang where puddles of fog lapped through the deep, jungled valleys below. They gave way to a prospect of shadowy lakes and islands and, peering out, I noted that the Boeing was cruising just beneath a filmy layer of stratus so shallow that its tail must have been cutting through the top like the fin of a shark.

My neighbour told me he suffered from recurring bunions and said the best remedies were available from Boots the Chemists in the U K. 'They have tip-top selection for feet disorders,' he added, 'so when I go to Britain I stock up. I have been many times. I look after overseas student welfare and we have 60,000 Malaysians studying there. My favourite place is Glasgow. That is a hot town!'

The flaps were extended with their coffee-grinder noise and the 737 descended over fields of burnt rice stubble towards the single runway at Sultan Abdul Halim airport. As it touched down the sun broke through heavy cloud and washed the blackened landscape in an eerie crimson light. Thirty or forty red-and-white Swiss-built Pilatus Turbo-Trainers were parked on the far side of the field where five platoons of uniformed boys and girls marched up and down, doing their early-morning drill before dashing off to school.

The drive into town took half an hour. I had hit the morning rush hour and, as we inched through the fashionable new contraflow and one-way systems my driver made his own prolonged contribution to the Alor Setar concerto for two-tone horns and broken silencers. At the high-rise Merlin Hotel everyone was having breakfast and, while waiting for a room to be vacated and cleaned, I asked the desk clerk if Alor Setar possessed a museum. He said yes, it had a *State* Museum and invited me to call its curator, Mrs Nabihah, from the lobby phone. Mrs Nabihah sounded brisk and friendly but regretted that her museum contained nothing about the airfield during the pre-war years. 'It is a big omission,' she said. 'I am jolly interested in aviation matters and I will have to do something about this. Perhaps there are some photographs or artefacts you would like to contribute yourself?' I told her that, unfortunately, I had nothing worth displaying and asked if there was anyone in Alor Setar who could help me. She suggested I call Mr Azizan, the present Airport Director. He was young, of course, but he might know something.

Mr Azizan said he would be delighted to meet for a talk. I was at the Merlin? He would be there when he came off duty, at 1400 hours. At 1350 hours he came bounding up the steps, a plump, energetic man with a wispy moustache who told me, as we sat in the coffee shop, that he was the first Malay to manage the airport. He came from Pulau Langkawi, an island just off the coast where the government were building a giant billion-pound tourist complex with an airport that would take 747s from all over the world. Mr Azizan indicated that one day he would like to go home and manage that. 747s! The largest visitor he had welcomed to Alor Setar had been a stretched DC9 on a sales demo, flown by an American astronaut. I asked him which astronaut and he shrugged. 'Not big-league fellow, I think, not a moon walker or anything like that.' He drank a Coke and said Mrs Nabihah had called and told him I was an important aviation historian. I laughed and pointed out that I was just an itinerant scribbler hunting for historians myself.

He persisted. 'Well, she think you know about the old days out at Sultan Abdul Halim.'

I ordered another coffee and shared my meagre store of facts with him. He hadn't heard that Imperial and KLM called here for fuel and provisions while travelling along the original trunk route between Bangkok and Singapore. Nor did he know of the occasion in 1931 when the *Southern Sun*, an Avro Ten of Australian National Airways (the airline founded by Sir Charles Kingsford Smith), crashed here on 25 November with mail bound for Britain. KLM offered to take it on but some Little Englander in the local post office declined on the grounds that their Fokker flew the wrong flag; patriotism, to the servants of the Empire, came before punctuality. So poor Kingsford Smith had to hasten up from Sydney in the *Southern Star* and carry the delayed cargo all the way to Croydon. There he picked up the Australian-bound Christmas mail and raced home with such a wind at his back that, characteristically, he broke the record *again*. The Alor Setar aerodrome then was a reclaimed paddy field, notoriously marshy, though the racecourse could be used by pilots caught short when the field was waterlogged.

And that, I said, was more or less the sum total of my local knowledge, except for the Tweezer Man.

'Excuse me?' murmured Mr Azizan.

I explained that he had been employed to pick dead insects out of the engines. Malaysian airspace teems with them and the old Atalantas, droning along at insect height, sucked them up like Hoovers. At Alor Setar he propped a ladder against the wing and painstakingly cleaned up the four Armstrong-Siddeley double Mongoose ungeared air-cooled radials, ridding them of the milled remains of dragonflies, moths, beetles, flying spiders, lacewings, fireflies, locusts, butterflies – including the great rainbow-coloured Malaysian swallowtails – perhaps even migrating booklice, all tweaked out by the Tweezer Man until the grass beneath would have glittered with iridescent fragments like the sweepings from a gem cutter's shop.

Mr Azizan said he would like to show me his airport. It was a fine sunny afternoon. He drove a new Honda and, as we negotiated the traffic systems, told me he was a fan of all things Japanese. An airport-management course in Japan had only served to increase his respect. The one thing the Japanese couldn't do was cook. Their food, he said, was so bad it had made him ill. We cleared the town centre and went bowling past the Kompleks Tunku Jaacob, a new shopping mall, and out into the open country, humming along under a huge Vermeer sky speckled with clumps of drifting cloud and several droning Pilatus Turbo-Trainers. Mr Azizan shared the field with the Royal Malaysian Air Force flying school but all

43

air-traffic duties were carried out by his civilian staff. 'Our ATC people are the best-qualified in South-East Asia. They must all have good degree, plus excellent health and hearing and 20–20 eyesight with good colour vision. Also clear speech, good English and quick thinking.' He pulled out to pass a bullock cart laden with oil drums. 'Last year I almost lost one. I sent him by Airbus from Penang to Kuala Lumpur on educational flight but the plane crashed 1,000 feet short of the K L runway. He survive okay but when he got back he said, "Hey, boss, what sort of education you trying to give me?"'

He laughed and identified the racecourse, deserted but for two men hitting golf balls down the home straight. 'My total staff is 180, including security personnel who have special training at Penang College. All luggage is now X-rayed *twice*. This has been the rule since a 737 with our Minister of Culture aboard explode just after taking off from Penang.'

We passed a handsome villa standing in a large, shadowy garden. 'That is home of the P M, Datuk Seri Dr Mahathir Mohamad. Before going into politics he was a local G P. Recently the Foreign Minister visited us here too. He was also in a bad crash recently. He is qualified pilot and his Piper 28 came down in the jungle, killing his co-pilot and bodyguard. To get help he had to walk for some days, eating only nuts and wild fruit.'

I observed that Malaysian politicians seemed to lead eventful lives. He said gravely, 'Oh, they are real get-up-and-go people. When the Airbus crash at K L the P M himself was there within a few minutes, helping the rescuers, treating the injured. My chap saw him working in the wreckage and thought, "My God, isn't that the PM?" but he wasn't surprised. In Malaysia we expect such things.'

The road, long and straight, ran past dense plantations of rubber trees. Mr Azizan turned off towards the terminal, a spacious new building set in a pretty tropical garden where, among beds of orange cannas, an elderly piston-engined Provost trainer sat on a plinth with vines growing around its wings. The restaurant, commanding a view of the empty tarmac, was full of families gossiping over soft drinks and plates of cakes. Mr Azizan said, 'The airport is a very popular place for outings. People like to see the planes and equipment. Here they can see that Malaysia is at the forefront of technology. It makes them feel good.' He went to the counter and bought a couple of Cokes. The girl attendants had been slouching and yawning when we entered and, though they now affected a great show of industry, the Cokes they gave us were warm. Mr Azizan frowned and spoke to them sharply, telling them to call the engineer – busted refrigerators had no place here on Malaysia's technological front line.

The late-afternoon sky turned silvery. To the south big lavender clouds were massing, heavy with the promise of rain. A small object suddenly emerged from them which, as it came curving towards us, assumed the dumpy profile of a 737. Mr Azizan glanced at his watch and noted approvingly that it was two minutes early. 'Inbound from KL,' he said. 'In half an hour he will return there then, after dark, he will come back to operate the night economy flight.'

The 737 drifted up to the threshold of Runway O4, breasting the breeze like a gull, and dropped gently, the thunder of its 45 reverse thrust booming around Sultan Abdul Halim like a tropical storm. We returned to the Honda. Mr Azizan had discovered that I had never looked closely at a rubber tree and, determined to put that to rights, set off at high speed past small kampongs, translucent bamboo groves, meandering brown creeks and pools with wild water lilies floating on them. We drove through the shadow of Bukit Tinggi, a lofty, jungle-covered volcanic plug rearing high above the plain like an inverted yoghurt tub. 'Bad place,' remarked Mr Azizan. 'Full of snakes. But men go up there to cut the stone. We call it Hill 450; that is its height in feet.'

This would have been the primary landmark for Imperial's pilots, I reflected, craning to gaze up its perpendicular sides but, by the same token, a real hazard in dirty weather. Then, four miles beyond, we coasted to a halt beside a plantation and strolled through dense, shadowy trees while Mr Azizan pointed out the lateral scarring where the trunks had been slashed to collect latex. Most of the trees had their cups in position for nocturnal milking. The plantation was thickly carpeted with damp russet leaves, like an autumnal English wood. Mr Azizan urged me to touch the bark. Wasn't it a miracle that a mere plant could produce such wealth? The nation had been built on its sap. As we returned to the car the 737 went racing overhead on its way back to Kuala Lumpur, the roar of its Pratt & Whitneys agitating hundreds of birds that had been roosting quietly in the treetops.

Driving home through the gloaming he confessed he never imagined he would ever become a person of such consequence. Airport Director, Alor Setar! Malaysia was a country where hard work and single-mindedness paid off. He socialized with the town's top people. He went to their houses, they came to his. 'What unites us is service to the community. That is what matters today.'

The road took us past the palatial residence built for the British District Administrator, now used for housing visiting VIPs, and then the old Planters' Club, an imposing structure looming massively in the dusk. We popped in for a look. The tuans had been replaced by wealthy Muslim teetotallers but the air still seemed scented with the whiff of gin pahits, shag tobacco and Capstans, and the talk still dealt obsessively with world rubber prices – which, Mr Azizan remarked as we slipped out again, were going through the floor. Back in the urban contraflow system we passed two remarkably ornate Edwardian timber structures, the Theatre Royal and the Empire, the former now condemned, the latter serving as a cinema. Here companies of travelling players had performed their Gilbert and Sullivan, their operettas and musical comedies. At the stage doors mooning young expats would have waited with armloads of orchids for the chorus-line blondes from *No, No, Nanette* and *The Sheik of Araby*.

We drew up at the Merlin. Mr Azizan had given up a large part of his day for me, but became gruff when I thanked him and shook hands. I took the elevator, marked '*lif bomba*', to my room, switched on the television and watched a recording of Brighton playing Liverpool in the Fourth Round of the F A cup, a match held in thin, wintry English sunshine. Brighton won 2–0. That was followed by an ad for Darkie toothpaste. I watched a smiling Malaysian family scrubbing their teeth in unison, then went down to the coffee shop for supper. A startlingly good-looking girl sat alone at the next table, eating a banana split and scowling over a paperback called *Guerrilla Tactics in the Job Market*.

At 0835 the MAS 737 climbed away from Sultan Abdul Halim through a hazy, overcast morning. Though the sky looked tranquil it was full of strange, conflicting currents that made the plane pitch and wallow. The paddy fields far below looked like complex, beautiful mosaics of mirrors and Roman glass. A smooth young banker in the next seat said the flight would last forty-five minutes and take us past Taiping, Ayer, Telok Anson and across the Slim River. He had made it several times. The bank paid, of course. For them it was a legitimate business expense and therefore tax-deductible. Then, without preamble, he said, 'Have you ever seen Mrs Thatcher, sir? In the flesh?'

'Only from a distance.'

'She is my ideal lady. She is my pin-up.'

I looked at him uneasily.

'I admire so much. Such leadership! Such courage! And that yellow hair – she is quite dishy, I would say. In Malaysia we think she is definitely the bee's knees.' He lit a Cabin 85 cigarette with a flash gold lighter. 'It is my ambition to go to London to study law, sir. When I come back I will be able to charge 160 dollars Malaysian for my signature!' He gave a sudden yelp of laughter. 'That is what people must pay a British-trained man for putting his name on a document. One six oh dollars!'

Half an hour later we began our descent over a battlefield of ravaged red earth and flooded pits. I asked my friend what was going on down there.

'They are sluicing for tin,' he said. 'The profits are good but it damage the soil, sir. For years afterwards the land is dead. Tin is all very fine but we cannot eat it.'

'I'll bet Mrs Thatcher can,' I said.

He gave me an uncertain smile. I looked down on a great dog's leg of devastated wasteland reaching away through the trees and far up into the hills like a colossal motorway project. It slipped astern and was replaced by a vast palm oil plantation. Here and there in the endless, orderly rows of trees there were small clearings containing houses on stilts; beside one a man was climbing on to a bare-backed horse and, as we came over, the horse reared up and the man jumped off again.

'All the rubber men want to get into palm oil now,' my friend remarked. 'They are coming to see us at the bank. They speak only of palm oil. It is where the smart money is going.'

Moments later, on finals, we skimmed over a dense tract of jungle with the patina of a tapestry worked in matching shades of green silk. 'That is specially protected land,' said my friend. 'Only experts in jungle studies are allowed to enter for research and surveys.' There was a clearing down there too, only a few miles from the perimeter of Subang, the Kuala Lumpur airport, with a venerable stilted house standing in its centre, fashioned from weathered thatch and smoky grey wood. Here, presumably, the jungle-studies experts lived, surrounded by the huge, silent trees of the rain forest, and I thought it looked the ideal 49 retirement spot, secluded and peaceful, until I remembered that the thundering noise footprint of our Pratt & Whitneys must be rattling the old building like a tambourine.

We touched down on Subang's 11,397-foot runway with its circling guidance lights and parallel crash strip (pilots inbound with a bad Mayday situation were expected to dump their wreckage in the space provided) and, moments later, I was past the *Kounta Transit*, out of the airport and heading down a broad new motorway in an air-conditioned Toyota *teksi*. Kuala Lumpur is a handsome city cradled in green hills but the combative nature of its traffic jams made the Alor Setar morning rush hour seem as well-mannered as a vintage car rally. I booked into a hotel with a view of the Racecourse then headed for the Far East Freight Conference Association offices. They were within walking distance and, on the way, I bumped into the French tour leader who boarded the Thai Airways 737 at Hat Yai. He had just shipped his Germans home and was in high spirits. Also, the previous evening he managed to wangle himself an invitation to some high-powered reception for senior tourism executives where, to his delight, he had met the King. 'In this country he is the ultimate contact,' he told me.

'What's he like?'

'He is a very good egg,' said the Frenchman.

We shook hands and I hurried on to keep my appointment with Mr William Cook, an exceedingly amiable Far East hand of the old school who, before the war, worked for Mansfield's in Singapore. The company's interests had ranged from ownership of shipping fleets and the Singapore Steam Laundry to the agency for Imperial Airways.

Mr Cook consulted his watch. 'Let's chat over a spot of lunch,' he said. 'We'll go to the Dog.'

He summoned his driver and, in the car, said his youthful Singapore posting had been a very agreeable period of his life which had been terminated by the arrival of the Japanese forces. Before the city fell Mansfield's used the old Imperial pinnace – by then the property of a brand-new corporation named BOAC, which had absorbed Imperial on April Fool's Day, 1940 – to ship refugees across the Malacca Straits to Sumatra. Some of Mansfield's own people got away in the last boatload. 'Frank Lane, the MD, was aboard, and so was Oliver Holt, a major shareholder and well-known local eccentric. Oliver loathed commerce and gave it all up to devote himself to Malay scholarship and a pretty little nutmeg plantation on the coast.'

The car pulled up beside a spacious, comfortable-looking white building which, despite a climate that attacks bricks and mortar like flame throwers and water cannon, had clearly stood there for a very long time.

'Here we are,' said Mr Cook, hopping out and leading me briskly indoors and up the stairs to the Long Bar. 'The Selangor Club, otherwise known as the Dog.' He ordered pink gins. 'It was founded a hundred years ago and has been a great KL institution ever since. The Prince of Wales came here in 1922 and scandalized everyone by dancing all night with a beautiful Eurasian girl from Ceylon. Every year there was a great ball on St George's Day when they carried in enormous sides of roast beef surrounded by blocks of ice with red roses frozen inside.' Mr Cook pointed to a balcony overlooking the *padang*, 51 as trim and green as Lord's. 'And Noël Coward wrote *Mad Dogs and Englishmen* while sitting there watching a game of cricket.'

Our drinks finished, we processed slowly to our table, Mr Cook pausing to greet the occupants of all the other tables passed in transit. He greeted the waiter with equal warmth and, when starched napkins had been draped across our laps like vestments, said, 'I never flew with Imperial, I'm afraid. As far as I know the only person left in KL who did is a chap called Tan Sri Dato Mubin Sheppard. He's an Irish Muslim who's been out here since 1928. Before he embraced the faith and took his new name – Mubin means Mervyn – his middle initial was ff. Stood, I think, for ffolkes. So everyone calls him fuffuff. Not to his face, of course, but people will say, "Seen old fuffuff recently?" or "fuffuff was in jolly good form last night". He and I usually meet here for a curry lunch on Sundays and I happen to know he once went to Southampton on an Imperial flying boat. I imagine his recollections will be similar to everyone else's – sitting in a noisy old machine barging through the middle of the cu-nim at 9,000 feet and always finding the most interesting storms.'

We ate magnificent chicken curries washed down with cold Tiger beer and talked about mutual acquaintances and the decline of manners and moral standards in Britain. It was a conversation the Dog had heard many times before – indeed, I had the uneasy feeling that everyone else in the dining-room was having it as well.

Later, back at my hotel, I called Tan Sri Dato Mubin Sheppard and asked if I could come and see him. But he said he was wrestling with the constitution of one of the many local societies he chaired; the members, against his advice, wanted the rules changed that very evening and he had a fight on his hands. Could I pop round in the morning? I explained that I had to catch an early plane to Singapore and suggested we talk on the phone instead.

'By all means!' he said in a surprisingly warm and youthful voice. 'Aren't you the chap who's interested in Imperial Airways? Bill Cook said you'd probably be in touch. I went on one of their flying boats. Did he tell you? From Colombo to Southampton after the war. Was it Imperial then?'

'BOAC,' I said.

'Oh, well, same lot, different nomenclature. Anyway, it was one of their *boats*, very spartan with its wartime decor, and dreadfully bumpy. They spilled my drinks all the way home. Usually we impoverished civil servants went P & O but I'd been delayed and had to get back in a hurry. The Japanese had locked me up for the duration – I was in Changi camp and then put to work on the railway – and several members of the Kempeitai, their military police, had given us a specially bad time. After the Surrender I heard they'd done a bunk to a little island off the Sumatra coast, so I thought I'd fetch them back to face the music. It took three separate expeditions and I missed the last of the ships going home with the POWs. When I failed to show up my wife started firing off messages asking where on earth I'd got to, so they put me on an aeroplane. We landed on the Nile, I believe.'

'Yes?'

'I haven't been the *slightest* help to you,' he said cheerfully   53 and, realizing that his interest in aviation matters was minimal, I asked about his adopted names.

'They're actually titles, old man. Tan Sri is an ancient one conferred by the Sultans on their chiefs. The first Prime Minister, Tunku Abdul Rahman, whose biography I have just completed, reinstated them for people who had performed a worthwhile service to the state. Tunku is the highest title, the equivalent of an earldom, while Dato is the third-ranking one. I've got two Datoships, probably for organizing the National Museum after independence and writing a lot of books about Malaysia. My field is the decorative arts and crafts – one of my books won a Gold Medal at the Italian Book Fair – but I've also brought out my autobiography. It's called *Memoirs of an Unorthodox Civil Servant*. The other thing perhaps you ought to know is that I'm eighty.'

At five o'clock that evening Kuala Lumpur was struck by a terrific tropical storm. Thunder boomed over the city and bounced back off the hills while gunflash lightning made the dense monsoonal rain eerily luminous. Across the street a deep pit dug for the foundations of an office block was filling like a bath. Cars inched by with foaming brown water swirling over the bottoms of their doors. A wind sprang up and, on the Racecourse, waves began breaking. Then, like a monstrous band marching off into the distance, the storm gradually faded away, leaving the mauve hills capped with cloud and wreathed in mist. From my vantage point Kuala Lumpur seemed so full of trees that it looked like a city camouflaged against the possibility of air attack. It was a pretty place and I would like to have stayed longer, but it wasn't one of my primary stops and I was obliged to hurry on. Between now and the end of my journey in Brisbane I had twenty-five more planes to catch.

An A300 Airbus was assigned to work M H 603 down to Singapore. Only a couple of dozen passengers boarded on this buoyant, sunny Saturday morning. After take-off a morose stewardess in a tight batik uniform brought me coffee and a little carton marked *krim*. As the red-and-green country slid by below I looked through *Wings of Gold*, MAS's glossy inflight magazine. The cover story was about Malaysian birds like the Asian Paradise Flycatcher, the Treepie and the Fire-tufted Barbet, while the Customs Information section advised incoming travellers that among the items exempted from duty were 'Not more than 100 matchsticks' and 'Not more than one pair of footwear'. A useful six-language double-page spread entitled 'Getting By in the Orient' taught me that 'aeroplane' in Bahasa Malaysia is *kapalterbang* (in Japanese it's *hikoki*, in Tagalog *eroplano*), 'bank' is *bank*, 'book' is *buku*, 'bus' is *bas*, 'coffee' is *kopi* and 'hello' is *hello*. It's *hello* in Tagalog as well.

When the stewardess came to collect my cup I thought of singing, 'You're the krim in my kopi,' but she gave me such a truculent look that I let it pass and turned back to *Wings of Gold*. The 'What's Up Doc' column posed a complex sequence of questions. 'Whenever you travel by air do your ears go "pop" or does your world go round and round? Do your ears ache or your eyes water? And do you suddenly find yourself farting and belching, much to your embarrassment and to the annoyance of your fellow-passengers?' If you suffered from any of these symptoms it was because the gas-filled cavities of your body were responding negatively to high-altitude travel. Gas in the gums can cause toothache, in the intestinal tract acute stomach pains; thus anyone prone to flatulence should avoid 'beans, cabbages, turnips and brussels sprouts' before a flight since, at 33,000 feet, they were likely to blow the victim up as explosively as a self-inflating dinghy. I read an item claiming that the 'French empress, Marie Louise, could move her ears at will, even turning them inside out', and then put the magazine away. Its name derives from the fact that MAS – Malaysian Airline System – is also the Bahasa Malaysia word for 'gold', a happy coincidence made much of by the company's copywriters. Had they been true to the economic realities of the country, of course, their title would have made reference to wings of rubber or tin.

Our route took us past Seremban and Malacca, then down along the coast over Batu Pahat and Johor Bahru. The A300 rode easily through calm air and a sky cloudless but for a range of cumulus stacked up on the eastern horizon; we cruised almost four times as high and nearly five times as fast as the Atalantas that had travelled the route half a century earlier. They had been introduced in 1933, specially built by Sir W. G. Armstrong Whitworth Aircraft Ltd for Imperial's operations throughout the tropical regions of the Empire and were, according to the *Gazette*, 'a high-wing unbraced monoplane type, equipped with four Armstrong-Siddeley double Mongoose air-cooled engines, of 340 horse power. The specification prepared by Imperial Airways demanded that the *Atalanta* class should have a cruising speed of 118 miles an hour, with an ability to maintain a height of 9,000 feet with any one of the four engines stopped, while carrying a paying load of 3,000 lbs – well over a ton and a quarter.' Each aircraft could accommodate a captain, first officer, wireless operator and nine passengers. 'One of the leading decorators in Great Britain' had been responsible for the passenger cabin. It had tilting chairs and soundproofing. The windows were 'large and made of safety glass. Each aeroplane is provided with a lavatory. The luggage and freight space is situated between the passenger cabin and the Captain's control cabin, and there is a special compartment for the stowage of the Mail.' The aircraft was also provided with hat racks and a sliding roof.

As we began our descent through scattered wisps of cloud the skipper switched on his P A and gave us a chatty, protracted discourse on the Singapore weather which, by now, we could see perfectly well for ourselves. We drifted over blue bays and islands, and saw the causeway bisecting the Johore Strait like a ruled line; the sun caught the windshields of cars making the crossing, Malaysians coming to Singapore for their Saturday shopping, Singaporeans escaping to spend the weekend on Malaysian beaches. Johore Bahru, at the mainland end, was a random scattering of highrise buildings. Away to the right Sumatra, huge and misty blue, loomed like a continent. The flaps and wheels went down, the cabin music system came on and we swept in low over Changi beach, its offshore water stained with effluent, and landed gently at Changi International.

READ MORE IN PENGUIN

For complete information about books available from Penguin and how to order them, please write to us at the appropriate address below. Please note that for copyright reasons the selection of books varies from country to country.

IN THE UNITED KINGDOM: Please write to *Dept. EP, Penguin Books Ltd, Bath Road, Harmondsworth, Middlesex UB7 0DA.*

IN THE UNITED STATES: Please write to *Consumer Sales, Penguin USA, P.O. Box 999, Dept. 17109, Bergenfield, New Jersey 07621-0120.* VISA and MasterCard holders call 1-800-253-6476 to order Penguin titles.

IN CANADA: Please write to *Penguin Books Canada Ltd, 10 Alcorn Avenue, Suite 300, Toronto, Ontario M4V 3B2.*

IN AUSTRALIA: Please write to *Penguin Books Australia Ltd, P.O. Box 257, Ringwood, Victoria 3134.*

IN NEW ZEALAND: Please write to *Penguin Books (NZ) Ltd, Private Bag 102902, North Shore Mail Centre, Auckland 10.*

IN INDIA: Please write to *Penguin Books India Pvt Ltd, 706 Eros Apartments, 56 Nehru Place, New Delhi 110 019.*

IN THE NETHERLANDS: Please write to *Penguin Books Netherlands bv, Postbus 3507, NL-1001 AH Amsterdam.*

IN GERMANY: Please write to *Penguin Books Deutschland GmbH, Metzlerstrasse 26, 60594 Frankfurt am Main.*

IN SPAIN: Please write to *Penguin Books S. A., Bravo Murillo 19, 1° B, 28015 Madrid.*

IN ITALY: Please write to *Penguin Italia s.r.l., Via Felice Casati 20, I-20124 Milano.*

IN FRANCE: Please write to *Penguin France S. A., 17 rue Lejeune, F-31000 Toulouse.*

IN JAPAN: Please write to *Penguin Books Japan, Ishikiribashi Building, 2-5-4, Suido, Bunkyo-ku, Tokyo 112.*

IN GREECE: Please write to *Penguin Hellas Ltd, Dimocritou 3, GR-106 71 Athens.*

IN SOUTH AFRICA: Please write to *Longman Penguin Southern Africa (Pty) Ltd, Private Bag X08, Bertsham 2013.*